LIFE TIME

LIFE TIME

A New Image of Aging

Photographs by Karen Preuss

Edited and Produced by Bill Henkin
Designed by Brenn Lea Pearson

Unity Press  Santa Cruz

Grateful acknowledgement is given to
Dr. Margaret Mead
for the use of material presented from her address
"What's Ahead for the Older American"

Published by
Unity Press
113 New Street
Santa Cruz, CA 95060

Preuss, Karen, 1939–
    Life Time.

    Bibliography: p.
    1. Aged—United States—Pictorial works.
2. Aging—Pictorial works.   I. Henkin, Bill.
II. Title.
HQ1064.U5P69   301.43'5'0973   78-1556
ISBN 0-913300-48-9

Printed in the United States of America

ACKNOWLEDGEMENTS

I would like to express my gratitude to a number of people for their roles in the conception and preparation of this book:

to Susan Molin, who first told me about SAGE after attending one of their workshops;

to Sharon Kaufman, who conscientiously recorded and transcribed all the weekly sessions of an entire year of SAGE, and who graciously made these transcripts available so that I could have the quotations that form the principal text of this book;

to Barbara Caley, who offered valuable suggestions during selection of the text;

to my husband, Paul, who encouraged me to pursue this project, and has continued to support and help me throughout;

to Bill Henkin, producer and editor, and Brenn Lea Pearson, designer, for their continuing interest and substantial efforts on behalf of *Life Time*, starting long before there was any assurance that it would ever be published.

I would also like to thank Ellen Bunning, who over the past three years has helped me find direction in my photography. Irwin Nash and Mary Randlett deserve special mention. They were my examples, my inspiration, and my first teachers at the time I became interested in documentary photography.

Finally, I would like to thank everyone at SAGE for welcoming me and allowing me to participate in their lives.

I would like particularly to talk about the need to develop a new style of aging in our own society, and to suggest that we could do more for the older American than we are doing at present. Everyone who is aging has a chance to develop this new style. Everyone who is working with old people can contribute to this new style.

—*Margaret Mead*

FOREWORD

The people in the photographs that follow are participants in groups and workshops organized by SAGE—Senior Actualizations and Growth Explorations—a group that is doing pioneering work in the field of gerontology in Berkeley, California.

I first heard about SAGE in 1975, from a social worker friend who was excited about the new approach the organization was taking in working with older people. As we talked, I saw the possibility for a photo essay that would be engrossing and informative, not only for people concerned with age and aging, but also for people involved with the human potential movement: that whole collection of philosophies and techniques designed to increase awareness of, and control over, one's life.

I photographed SAGE for more than a year. It was not only fascinating; it was also exciting to see people—some of whom were residents of nursing homes, senior residences, and similar institutions—changing, growing, and expanding their involvements with their own lives and the lives of the people around them.

The photographs in this book were taken during actual working sessions of SAGE: in their independent core groups, in a few institutions, and in the workshops SAGE sponsors for training people who work with the elderly. The text that accompanies the photographs was taken from transcripts of various SAGE sessions. Except for the group's co-directors (Gay Gaer Luce, Eugenia Gerrard, and Ken Dychtwald), participants are identified only by fictitious first names, in order to protect their privacy. A few of the exercises used in SAGE core group sessions and a brief essay about SAGE appear in the appendices at the end of this book.

Karen Preuss
San Francisco
February, 1978

A NEW IMAGE OF AGING

There is a widespread myth in American culture that older people cannot change. We think of childhood as our period of growth; the middle years are our period of power, when we use the abilities we've developed in our youth; and old age is left for "retirement"—the time to stop, and to remove ourselves from the mainstream of society.

It is no surprise that in this culture the elderly are tolerated rather than revered, and that they often see themselves as we—and they—have been conditioned to see them. But what we accept as cultural myth is not necessarily the truth.

In some cultures, the stage of life we call "retirement" is seen as an opportunity to examine all the experiences a person has accumulated during the early and middle years of his or her life. It is seen as a time when new possibilities become available for self-development, a time for learning new skills. It is also seen as a time when the wisdom acquired during earlier years can be passed on to the younger generations, enriching their sense of history and social continuity.

In those cultures, older people do not suffer the isolation, loneliness, and degradation to which we frequently subject them in ours. There, increased age does not mandate a limit to self-development or to social participation, partly because the functions fulfilled by older people are both clear and vital to the prevailing social fabric, and partly because old age itself is estimable, and not shameful.

In our culture, we are encouraged to derive our sense of self-worth largely from what we do in the world, whether this entails working at home raising children or working in an office or factory at a salaried occupation. When a person's work cycle is completed—ordinarily by the early or mid-sixties—very little remains to affirm his or her self-image. Thus a large, potentially active, and highly competent segment of our population is coerced into feeling that it is not needed, or wanted, any longer.

That we seek to remove these people from our immediate environment, by law and by social pressure, bespeaks the poverty of our social imagination, as well as the magnitude of our own culturally ingrained fears of becoming old, outmoded, and displaced.

I began to work on this book in my mid-thirties, at an age when, like many other people in my generation, I was just beginning to be aware of the problems of aging. Partly, my awareness was provoked by an experience common to us all—that of each year passing conspicuously faster than the last. Yet, I also had a perspective that was somewhat unusual. My parents were older than those of my contemporaries, and therefore seemed to me to change very little as I grew older. There was no dramatic change, never a moment when I said to myself, "Now they are old."

By contrast, I was that much more aware that my friends' parents and grandparents did change. The contrast was heightened as I observed the difference between my father and other older people. He was a university professor who worked until the day he died, at the age of seventy-eight. I never noticed in him the drastic changes I saw in others, the upheaval in life-style brought on by retirement.

With the exception of organizations such as SAGE and the Gray Panthers, I have seen little constructive attention paid to the process of creative aging. Although there are indications that our attitudes toward older people are beginning to change, our social posture with regard to older people remains even harsher than our stereotyped attitude toward children, who—according to the adage—should be seen but not heard. We would rather not even have to look at the elderly, much less listen to them.

The first time I entered a nursing home I was afraid. Mine was an irrational fear, but real nevertheless. The source of my fear is simple, I believe, and true for many people: we are afraid of what may become of us. Even the best-run convalescent hospitals are all too often the homes of the abandoned, the useless, the unwanted.

I have seen people forced into retirement while still vital and energetic, deprived of the challenges that gave meaning to their lives, abruptly unable to fill the empty hours. Some are swallowed up by the shame of retirement and the stigma attached to no longer being "productive." Illness, drug dependence, and alcoholism find them easy prey.

I would like those people—and those of us who may face our own version of that crisis sooner than we think—to know that it doesn't have to be that way. Many older people experience satisfaction with their lives, experience change in fulfilling ways, contribute meaningfully to our society both actively and contemplatively, and do not allow themselves to be ostracized. I believe many more can share in these riches. Someday, we may all be able to share them. The choice is ours.

We can learn much from those who are growing older. Perhaps the most important lesson they can teach us is that their growth is no different than our own. Growth only stops when we choose to stop it.

Partly, this book is intended to let you, the reader, glimpse the development of the SAGE project, and thus share an experience of what it can be like to be vitally alive in old age. What I saw changed my view, and I have tried, through these photographs, to carry some of my new vision to you. But primarily, I hope this book will help dispel the prevailing myths about old age, and show that all of us can live full and healthy lives in which we never stop growing. For growth is the nature of human life itself.

Karen Preuss

CORE GROUPS

I think this should be the most beautiful part of your life, because you have the freedom to do exactly as you please. For me, it's better now than it ever was.

I think part of my difficulty has to do with my feeling that I'm not in any period. I'm young enough not to categorize myself as old, but I'm old enough that I can't quite think of myself as young. It's as if part of me is ready to settle for the last quarter of life, but a large part of me is saying No.

I feel that I belong to the segment of the population that is growing and learning about new things. I'm doing things that some people think are far-out, weird, and so forth. But I have the feeling that I'm enlarging my outlook. It has nothing to do with whether I accept these things or not. As the kids say, I'm hep.

Eugenia: *It occurred to me that the people at Brentwood's Rest Home* can't *get out and give anything to anybody else. They're really confined. They come up against meaninglessness even if, at one time in their lives, they did give a lot, because now there are no possibilities for giving out. They are very restricted. I've been thinking for myself that I would like to look forward to the last part of my life as a time when I really go inward, and have that be meaningful. I would like to look forward to it, and gear my life to it. That makes sense to me.*

Alice: *It's a very revolutionary concept. You'd have the whole culture down on you.*

Mary: *That's it exactly.*

Alice: *They'd say there was something wrong, you shouldn't do that, you shouldn't sit in the house and read a book, or do your needlework. I'm not arguing with you, but I think that older people are made to feel—and this goes for anybody in the culture–that unless you are outward, then you'd better find out what's wrong with you.*

Gay: *We're taught that meaning is outside.*

Alice: *Yes. It has to be something that people can see you doing.*

Lilian: *But that's brainwashing.*

Eugenia: *I just realized that I really want to change things. I want to change the culture, because I want to get old feeling that there is a place for me to spend time on myself, some internal place.*

Betty: *I'm very selfish with my time, and I love to be alone, and I never have enough time being alone, though I am alone all the time. I love solitude.*

Jack: *In many Oriental cultures this is taken for granted, but I think they all emphasize that you need a technique to get inside. "Go inside," it's wishy-washy, doesn't mean much to most people. You need a technique.*

Eugenia: *It's a great gain to be practicing these techniques. But if you only take your twenty minutes a day to do them, it's not the same as taking the time to focus your life inward.*

Betty: *You can carry that over into your everyday world. I can get into that state and do the dishes or some other work. I can keep that state, sort of a serenity, as I go on doing what I want to do.*

Philip: *Eugenia's idea attracts me very much, just so it doesn't imply withdrawal. I don't think it does. I really think it might be the opposite, if one really does something for himself or herself. You take the time to look back and realize what principles have guided you and what things are meaningful and valuable. I think if I could be successful doing that, my communications with others might be all the better, because, in that sense, I would be surer of myself. It's like this quality of love. People who are really loving have an absolutely inexhaustible supply. I don't know why, but you can't exhaust it if it's genuine and it's there. So I think the more perception one has of oneself, the more one has to share with others.*

I come to a spot that's a very won-
derful spot. It's as though all of
a sudden, there's complete quiet,
both inside and outside. It doesn't
happen right away, but at a certain point it's just this feeling that
everything is standing still.

I'm very angry about getting older. I'm furious about it.

Henry was talking about some woman he was with recently, and used the words "sex appeal" with the obvious kind of comparison. I don't have that kind of sex appeal. And I'm enraged. It isn't just Henry. It's the recognition that this has been a monkey on my back from the time I was born, practically. That I was not pretty to begin with, and I'm not now—whatever the ideal measurements are— and I am just so angry about the values of our society, that here I am, still being measured in this very stupid, narrow way. I really get furious. And I'm getting nowhere with this man because I can't do anything about his concepts of value. He tries to get out of what he's saying by indicating what I could do to make the most of my attributes, and yet we have this different idea of beauty. The same thing must be true of aging. That our society has this fixed idea of age which is negative, and we're all victimized by it.

I think any age group has its problems, and I think the reason is that people don't have a functional place in our society today. The way culture evolved, children had a place, adolescents had certain rituals. And old people understood that they were important. You were the keeper of your society, of the laws, of the rituals, of the initiations, of the ceremonies, the history, and the oral tradition.

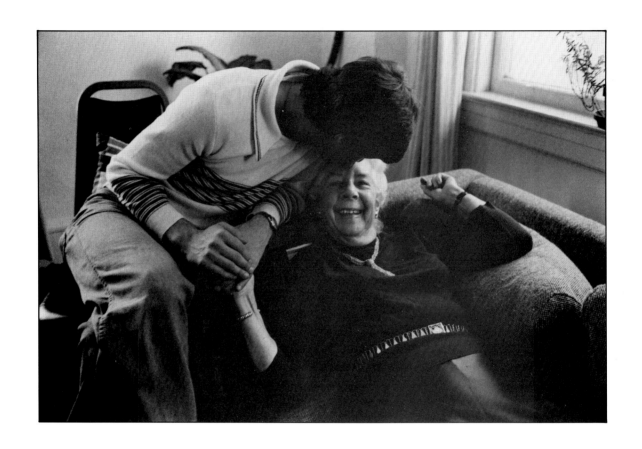

I think we've got to be careful not to suffer from self-inflicted wounds. I find young people very delightful. I don't find young people looking down at me. I get smiles now from young girls occasionally, and I know it's on account of my gray hair.

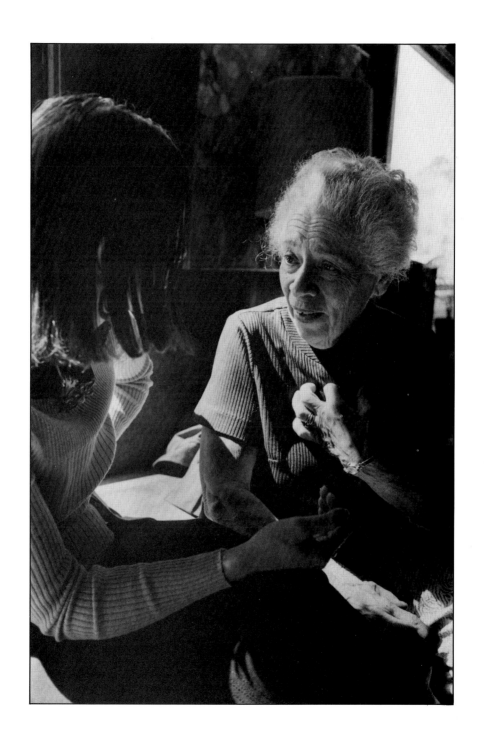

Most of my life has been goal-oriented. I thought I was supposed to be doing something, producing something, waiting for something. I've been thinking about that. I was thinking about an art teacher I had, maybe twelve years ago. She was trying to get me to relax into my painting. I was so busy drawing, trying to make it exactly perfect, that I hated doing it. I was so hung up on that end product. And she finally said, "This is the art, and the finished product is not art." Doing *is the art.*

Carolyn: *I have a question. I was at a crafts fair the other day, and a lady was doing massage. What is the purpose of a massage? Several people were standing in line, and I didn't know if I should go or not. Why massage? Is it so great? I was embarrassed to put my feet in the dishpan or whatever it was. But other people weren't.*

Gay: *The parts of the feet supply stimulation and healing to other parts of the body. So-called primitive people, who walk bare-foot all the time, are always stimulating their entire bodies. Massage is one way. If you think about it, what does a little kid do? He's always turning somersaults and standing on his head, and rolling— he's massaging his body all at once. Most illness begins to show up at college age and afterwards, when we are sedentary, because we aren't getting any stimulation. Massage, on the most primitive level, supplies some of that stimulation, therefore not only allowing the circulation and stimulation of the foot to improve, but improving the strength of the entire body.*

Paula: *And our feet are our only physical contact with being here on this planet. When you think about the link between the universe and Earth, it's our feet. We really should honor that.*

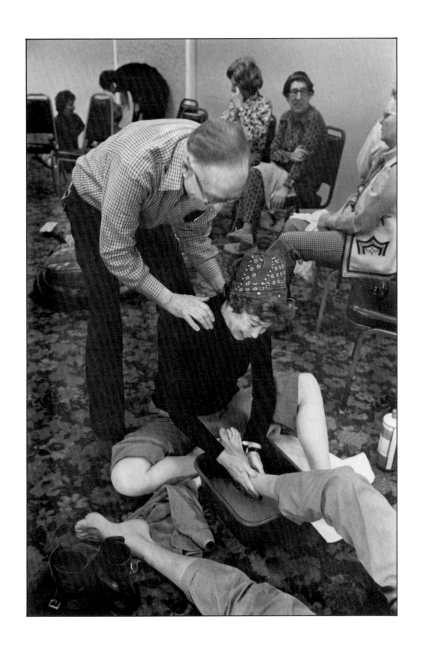

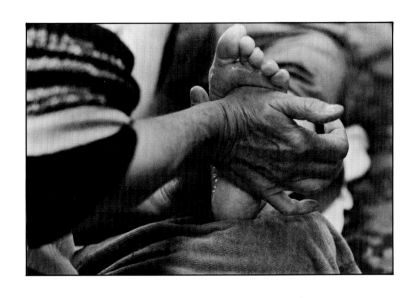

One thing I'm noticing lately is that we use other people as mirrors. I try to get feedback from people about the way they see me, to tell me who and what I am. Deep inside me, I know perfectly well—if I get in touch with it. And the more I get in touch with it, the less it matters. I look to other people as mirrors, as if I have nothing to go on. But I have a great deal to go on.

The role that I enjoy now with my children is when they come to me for my wisdom. I am fortunate in that they talk to me about the most private kinds of things. They express a great deal of love and appreciation, and I'm glad I'm the kind of mother who can do that. I'm also aware of the fact that in that role, helping them sort out their decision-making, their sexual problems, that's where I come alive.

INSTITUTIONS

Eugenia: *How do you recognize you're old? How does that feel?*

Evelyn: *One of the things that has forced me to recognize it is the memory loss I experience. As a reference librarian, it drives me nuts.*

Alice: *I make a joke of it. I say, "Ask me anything that happened thirty years ago, but not what happened yesterday."*

Anna: *I find that if it exasperates me, very rarely does it make any difference. The person I'm talking to isn't usually that interested anyway.*

Mary: *One of the positive things is that I'm not in the rat race where I have to remember all the little details I had to remember.*

Helen: *Yes. A lady in my movement class for older people told me that she thought her memory wasn't getting any worse, but that she was getting smart enough not to remember so much crap.*

Carolyn: *Oh, you're absolutely right! The things I had to remember—and now I can get rid of them all! Just marvelous. It's like having a vacation.*

Jack: *One way I can tell time goes by is to look in the mirror. I see marks from frowning, and wrinkles, and my hair is gradually changing from gray to white. It isn't as though I dislike what I see, but I wouldn't mind looking in the mirror and finding my reflection just the way it was when I was forty, or thirty, or twenty, or ten.*

Alice: *I can finally look in the mirror and see myself and know that it's me. Not anyone else. It doesn't bother me any more. It did.*

Abe: *If I look in the mirror and find any signs of aging, it's very disturbing.*

Eugenia: *When you say you're disturbed, what kinds of feelings come across you?*

Abe: *Anger.*

Mary: *I just had a thought: anger's the reason for my breathing problems. It prevents my ability to relax, and think in a calm manner.*

Eugenia: *How do you know you're old?*

Mary: *I know when I look in a mirror. It surprises me that my skin is a different color and texture. And lines. Sometimes it's not there. Sometimes I see in the mirror just what I feel inside. And sometimes it doesn't match at all. And it's very upsetting to me. It's a jolt, a distress.*

Lilian: *I thought of scrubbing my kitchen floor the other day, and I'm more than up to scrubbing the kitchen floor. But the brainwashing about "being older" was in there, and I didn't scrub it. It wasn't because I couldn't. It was simply an acceptance of a false kind of limitation.*

Jack: *There's an old Tao story about a man who is a hunchback, and he's lived alone for years and years. One day he walks in the mountains and passes a reflecting pond. And he hasn't seen any people who've told him he's old, or that he has a hunchback. He looks in this pond and sees his reflection, and he says, "Oh, how beautiful!"*

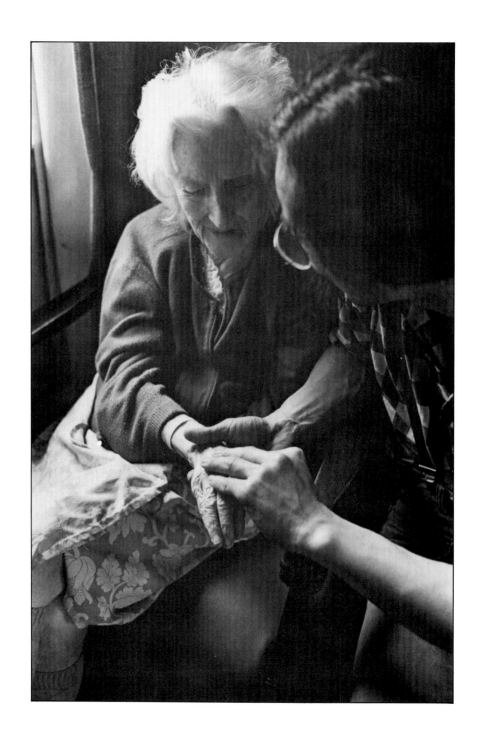

Since I've been here I've made peace with my being old. I look at myself and it's all right. But I do this for the first time in years. And I'm glad this transition has happened.

I think about my grandmother who was very, very senile when she died. She was so senile that she talked to me as "that man from Berkeley." It was very difficult for me to maintain contact with her. I thought, "She sure is degenerating, her brain cells and all of that." But one of the things a lot of young people are trying to do, and paying money for in workshops, is to experience altered time changes or multiple personalities. And she was there. [Laughter] Suppose we never knew the word "degenerate," that it just wasn't part of the language. Then when we observed someone who exhibited that kind of behavior, we would have to say, "Well, they are doing something I don't understand yet."

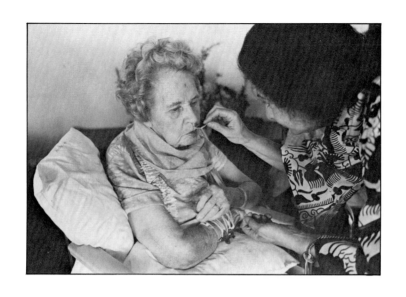

We do not really value the experience that shows in the faces and bodies of people as they're growing older. You cannot grow old gracefully even if you want to.

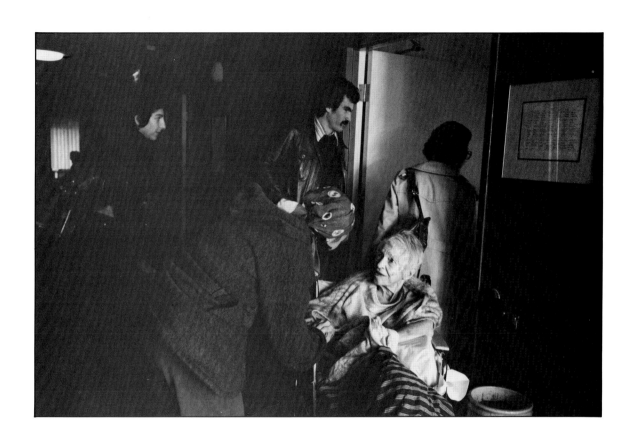

Eugenia: *What kinds of things have we done together that have begun to change your self-images?*

Helen: *That you people, who are young to me, are willing to spend time with us. It's a feeling that we're not discarded.*

Evelyn: *A supportive feeling, as if we're contributing something to your understanding.*

Mary: *That we have some value, and that you want this understanding.*

Alice: *There are so many new things happening, we can't really be part of them all. But we'd like to understand them, to be around young people and to understand what their feelings are. New life styles—we're out of this. But I'm very much interested in seeing this change go on, and I want to be part of the young people, and not have them feel, "You're just an old lady and you don't understand." I'd like to be able to be part of the community.*

Jack: *This whole group demonstrates that there is such a thing as growth and development, and it continues until you die. It's up to us to find the meaning in our lives. Nobody else can find it for us.*

I was walking by three little girls who got themselves into a tangle on the ground. As I came by, there was an image of me, and I was down there with those girls. What I did was to say, "Can I play too?" And they just giggled and giggled. And I didn't feel safe enough about my body to actually get down there with them, but I wouldn't have asked a year ago.

This morning I sat down and decided to worry, and a funny thing happened—my mind wouldn't let me worry.

Eugenia: *I'd like you to reach over and touch someone next to you and note that the person you're touching is old. Whether they are or not.* [*Quiet laughter*] *Keep your eyes closed and feel whether this person is old or not. See what comes to you.*

Lilian: *Immediately it came through that there is a fraud going on. She's not old, doesn't feel old at all.*

Abe: *I had an immediate feeling of strength.*

Helen: *I had a feeling of cherishing.*

Anna: *I had the feeling that Abe's being old was an illusion.*

Lilian: *In no way can I see Alice as old. In my body, or my mind, or my eyes.*

Alice: *I can't see Lilian as old either.*

Mary: *I can't with Carolyn.*

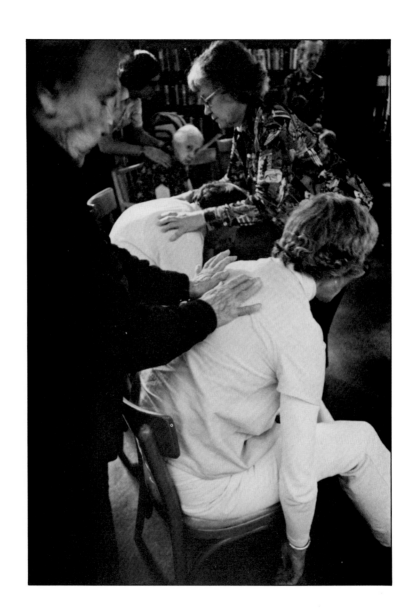

Carolyn: *I'm puzzled about one of your exercises. I've had a kink in my neck for two years, and with your exercises it went away. Before that I'd been to specialists and everything.*

Jack: *Oh, that happens all the time.* [*Laughter*]

We're really not afraid of death—at least, I'm not. But I'm afraid of something that might come before. Illness or something, so that you become dependent on someone. Death in itself is just beautiful. I'd like to think that it can be just a natural transition. I didn't always think so, but I do now. I'd like to prepare myself for that.

I went to visit my college roommate, whom I have known now for over fifty-five years. We had a couple of hours, we were sitting having a drink in the afternoon, and the phone rang. She took it in the other room. She came out with her hat and coat on and said, "My son is very ill, I have to go." She hadn't been gone fifteen minutes when the phone rang again and they said her son was dead. And I was left alone, in her house, with the memories of our recent conversation, and thinking back to when we were freshmen in college. My feeling was, she was a very brilliant girl, and very gifted, and in her early days I admired her for these things. But after all these years, and we've had our lives, I thought of her much more now as an understanding, giving, and tolerant person. I didn't think about her intellectual gifts, but of her personality—how beautifully it had developed, and how she was going to need everything she had to meet this situation.

WORKSHOPS

Mary: *I was reading Bettelheim's* Children of the Dream *the other day, and I thought that would be a great life for me now, on the kibbutz. Because the people are incorporated as part of this extended family, and I'm so completely alone here.*

Eugenia: *Really?*

Alice: *I think a commune is a good idea.*

Carolyn: *I do too. I would love it.*

Alice: *A commune where younger and older people would be together. I think sometimes that's the only solution.*

Mary: *All the generations. Not the isolation.*

Eugenia: *Would those of you who live alone really like to live on a commune? Is that a real alternative?*

Alice: *I would like to try it.*

Philip: *I would too.*

Abe: *Yes.*

Carolyn: *I would like to have my own room. But eat together, wash clothes together. I would like that.*

Ken: *We're not here expecting that all of you are Supermen and Superwomen, that you're going to do everything and try everything, or even like everything. Please don't think that's what we want. Don't force yourself. We're going to offer things. Tell us if you're nervous or upset, or if you don't want to participate. Don't make believe everything is good, because it's not.*

Lilian: *You picked up on something that's practically my life-time script: I can't say no.*

Carolyn: *Is it hard to learn to say no? It is hard, isn't it? You always think you're going to hurt the other person.*

Lilian [*agreeing*]: *You're going to be a bad girl.*

Eugenia: *Maybe we should do the exercise we do at Brentwood's Rest Home—everybody stomp on the floor and say "No!"*

Lilian: *I'm more comfortable with people who say no to me, because then I don't have to guess. People who let you know where they stand, you can be more comfortable with them. So I'm realizing for the first time that I've actually cheated people.*

I've been running around keeping busy, doing things that the world calls meaningful. The world has very high kudos for that. And I realize that, in my own life, they've been noise.

I noticed that a smile was appearing on my face. It was an unconscious thing. It took over almost by itself.

Ken: *Let's be in a circle and take a moment to see how each one of you, personally, feels right now. Take a look around the room and look at each person. I'd like for us to go around the room and I'd like each of us to say something—a reflection or a comment, something brief, anything you might like to share.*

Carolyn: *I feel lovely, and very much at peace.*

Philip: *I feel peaceful too, slowed down from when I first came in here. It feels good.*

Mary: *I have the feeling that each one is interested in each other. A great deal of trust in one another. That's a strong feeling.*

Lilian: *I feel two things. I feel related, and I feel that Mary has taught me a new sense of the meaning of trust.*

Evelyn: *Well, I've just been to the dentist, and I hurt. And I wasn't sure I was going to get here at all. And I feel fine that I got here.*

Jack: *I realize that I really look forward to coming to the group. I work in the morning so that I can come over in the afternoon.*

Anna: *I'm in touch with the peacefulness that I feel within myself, and that's surrounding me right now. It's nice.*

Helen: *This has been a very rewarding experience for me. It turned out to be very positive.*

Abe: *Well, I think that everybody is very supportive and honest. And I enjoyed my little experience with Betty. We talked a little bit, and we found ourselves both a little reticent. In terms of this past performance of putting your arms around somebody you don't really know, this slight intimacy, informal, going around holding them. Not that I didn't enjoy it, but I guess maybe I've been afraid to enjoy it or something. Because I'm not much about making advances to strangers.*

Betty: *I loved it.*

Ken: *Was it okay?*

Abe: *Yeah. Well, it was a little strange. I don't do that.*

Ken: *I want to say two things, and then we'll close the session. First, I want to honor you, and tell you how much I appreciate your willingness—just plain willingness and openness. One of the things we'd like to do is to give you some exercises that you can practice at home. An awareness of the subtleties of your own emotions is important. To approach it from a slow, conscious perspective is really satisfying.*

APPENDICES

APPENDIX A
SAGE Core Group Exercises

[*Note: These exercises were transcribed from an actual SAGE session. Comments in italics were made by participants in response to the group leader's instructions or questions.*]

Stand with your feet together and close your eyes. Start to put your attention inside your body, and begin to see how you do that. For instance, what colors are you when you put your attention inside your body? When you look inside yourself, do you see colors at all? Or how light or how dark you are? Don't try to make something up: you might not see colors, you might not experience things visually.

Notice what texture you are. Are you like French onion soup, or split pea soup, or beefsteak? What texture are you when you put your attention inside your body? What kind of experience is that? If you do not have a visualization, maybe you get sensations or feelings of some kind. For instance, if you think about your right hand, and you put your attention in your right hand, what happens? Do you see your right hand, or do you feel your right hand?

Travel through your body and see if you feel different textures. Maybe the right and left halves feel very different. They might be different colors. One side might be light, the other dark. If you're feeling nothing, try to see that. Certainly if your eyes are closed and you've got your attention inside your body, *something* is happening. What is it like for you to have your attention inside your body?

The first thing I experience is the coursing of blood, a kind of vibration. The color of French onion soup is all right, but the texture is granular.

When I go inside my body I feel my chest as black.

When you go inside your body, what is its density? Do you feel it to be a very light medium, or is it very thick and heavy?

The big parts of my body seem like a gray corduroy, but my hands feel like satin, they're a lighter color. I can see my speech organs in red, and boiled spaghetti for my brains.

Go inside your head with your attention. See what color and what texture your head is. What kinds of sensations do you get when you do that? Try not to think about how it *should* be, but find out what your raw experience is of having your attention inside your head. Now, quickly change from your head to your abdomen, and contrast the two. See if there's a difference.

This might be unusual for you. Maybe the experiences I'm describing don't convey the way *you* put *your* attention inside your body. You might feel as if you're not feeling anything. But you are. It's just that it might not be visual, and it might not be in terms of textures.

Experience how large you feel your head is inside. Try not to relate to how large you *know* it is, but find out what your experience is of the space inside your skull, in your nose, in the back of your head, between your ears, up and down. Just the sense of space, as though it were a room you just walked into.

Put your attention in your belly and do the same thing. What is your sense of space there: as though you opened a door somewhere around your diaphragm and walked into your belly.

It's larger than life in both cases, for me.

Now put your attention back in your head again, and let's do some neck rolls to increase the sensations of our heads.

Stand with your arms just hanging down. Make sure you're not holding onto anything. Very slowly let your head drop down and really look at the ground. Keep your eyes looking down toward your chin and roll your head very slowly toward the right side, as though you wanted to get your ear on your shoulder, and then look up toward the ceiling with your eyes. Really look up. Then go over to the left with your head, and down again.

All the while you're rolling your head, look around and see how much of the room you can see. Notice the space of the room around your body, and see if you can get your head to roll smoothly at the same time. You'll probably notice that it jerks a little as it goes around. Challenge yourself to roll it as slowly and smoothly as possible. How does your neck feel?

Mine is full of sand and gravel.

Go inside your head again and get that sense of spaciousness. Is there any difference between what your head feels like now and what it felt like before we did the neck rolls? Let's see if we can increase how far around we can roll our heads.

Stand with your arms straight out to your sides. Lower your right ear toward your right shoulder and see how close it comes. Raise your head back up again. Do that several times, until you really notice how close your right ear comes to your right shoulder. Lower your arms and rest.

Now, raise your right arm and attach your ear to your shoulder as if you had some glue dabbed to your earlobe, and you were going to glue it right to your shoulder. Keeping your ear glued to your shoulder, begin to lower your arm down toward your side, toward the ground, and then raise it toward the ceiling again. Do it slowly and don't strain.

Move your arm around in space. Begin to explore up, down. Wherever you move your arm, your ear stays on your shoulder. That's the game: that the ear has to stay on the shoulder. Let it be an easy movement; let your breathing be easy. See how low down you can bring your arm, down to your side, keeping your ear on your shoulder. Take a deep breath every so often, feeling your ribs expand. Then lower your arm and rest.

Just to see if this exercise has had any effect, hold your arms straight out to the sides again. Keep them in place and lower your right ear to the right shoulder and see if it can get any closer than it could before. See if you can get your ear on or close to your shoulder. Lower your arms.

Let's see if it happens on the other side. Take your left arm and glue your left ear to your left shoulder, and begin to move the arm down and up. Move it in all directions. See if you can make big circles in space with your left hand, keeping your ear glued to your shoulder. Breathe easily. Let your jaw drop open. Lower your arms and rest.

Hold your arms straight out to your side again, and put your left ear on your left shoulder. See if they come any closer than before the last exercise, and see if it's getting easier for you to move your head from side to side. Lower your arms. Just stand for a little while, and experience how your neck and your head feel. See if you feel more space opening up on the sides of your neck, or if you're more aware of that distance between your ear and your shoulder.

I lost some of the gravel. There's only sand now.

Let's try something with our shoulders now. Get a sense of your shoulders before you begin to move. That means your shoulder blades and your back. See if you can get a feeling for your shoulder blades—both of them. You might want to put your attention in your right shoulder and then in your left shoulder, to see if there's a difference between them. How big are they? Notice if it's easier for you to put your attention in one shoulder than in the other.

Since we started doing the exercises I've had a change in the feeling. At first the left side felt lower, and now it feels lower on the right side.

I had a tremendous sense when we started that I was lopsided. Now I feel good.

I'd like to remind you that the responsibility for stopping any exercise is on you. If you feel that your arms are out there too long, don't think you have to do it. You never learn anything when you're tired, and there's not any point in exercising unless we're having fun and we learn something about our bodies. If you feel fatigued or you feel a cramp coming on and you feel you *should* keep going, that's not fun any more, and your body doesn't want to pay attention to that area.

I'd like us all to sit down on the floor now. Put your feet straight out in front of you, and lean on your hands in back of you for support if you need to. Just let your legs be really limp. See if you can shake them. Hold onto your right knee, and lift it up and set it down and lift it up and set it down. Lift it higher now and set it down. See if you can make your leg absolutely limp, lifting it with your arms. See if you can find a way to get your leg to go back up just using your hands. See if you can move your right leg around completely limp, without any feeling that you're pushing it up or setting it down. Do this a few times, until you can really experience that leg not moving.

Hold onto your foot, or down closer to your ankle, and let your head look at what you're holding onto. Lift your foot, bend your knee a little, and lift your knee by holding your foot. Slide your leg back out again. When you slide it out, see that your knee gets straight. See if you can rock back and forth, building a kind of rhythm so that you can pull your foot up toward you and push it down away from you. Repeat.

If it's easy for you to hold onto your ankle, do so. Only hold onto what's comfortable to hold onto. Most people are going to hold onto their calf muscles, or maybe just a bit below their knees. Do whatever works for you. Now rock back a little bit, holding onto your foot or ankle or whatever. Keep holding on, and lift your foot up and move it around. Move it to the left and right, make a circle with it in the air, and set it back down again. Find a way to be comfortable, and see if you feel a difference between your two legs. Does one leg feel longer than the other? It's easiest to tell about that with your eyes closed.

Hold onto your left knee with your left hand and see if you can hold onto the ankle or calf muscle with your right hand. Bend your knee and pull your foot in toward you and slide it away from you. Let it be easy. Are you pressing your tongue into your upper mouth, or gritting your teeth? When your foot goes out, let your head go down. Let your head droop. When you pull up, look at the ceiling. Pick your foot all the way up in the air and move it 'way up toward the right, and then over toward the left. Imagine you had your heels resting on a table, and you were going to dust the table off with your foot.

Look with your eyes at the circle your foot is making in space, and see if in fact it's a circle, or if you're just sort of making a vague circular motion. And rest. Now get a sense of your legs. See if one feels longer than the other now. See which leg feels more attached to your body. See if you have a feeling of one leg maybe belonging to you a little more than the other one.

Now, lie on your backs. Draw your knees up so that your feet are flat on the floor. Raise your right knee up over your chest so that you can hold onto it with your hands, and very slowly pull that knee toward your chest just a little bit. Now pull it away. See that when your knee goes away from your chest it goes so far away that your arms become straight. Go back and forth with that several times. And let the foot down.

Draw both knees up over your chest, and put one hand on each knee and let your feet relax. Notice if your feet get tense when they're up there. Let them relax, let the toes droop down as much as they can. Notice as you're doing this that your back is shifting on the ground a little bit: your pelvis kind of rolls. If you're really rested when you're doing this, you might feel that your head begins to move because you're pulling on your knees. See if that bobbing action doesn't go right through the spine and make your head kind of nod up and down a little bit. Keep your head on the floor, rested back. While you're doing that, very slowly move your head from side to side. Very slowly. Let your jaws separate. And then let your feet go down and let your legs grow long. Just notice how your back feels on the ground. Put your attention back inside your body and see if it's changed in any way.

There's more circulation in my legs.
I feel less corduroy inside.

Draw your knees up above your chest one more time, and hold onto one knee with each hand, and pull your knees wide apart. Bob both knees toward your chest, one hand on each knee. See if you can let your feet go wide—don't keep them together. Let your head be completely at rest and stick your tongue out. With the bobbing action of your knees, roll your head from side to side, having your tongue lead the direction. Let it be very slow, almost as if your tongue is spilling your head from side to side. And rest. Put your attention inside your body and get a sense for the quality of how you feel.

Raise your left knee, and place your left foot flat on the floor. Raise your right foot up toward the ceiling. So you've not only raised your right knee above your chest, but you've put your foot toward the ceiling and you're holding on in back of your knee with both hands. Bend your leg if necessary. Very slowly bob that foot toward your head. Feel your arms moving your leg a little bit. Rest. Feel if there's any difference between your legs, and try to define for yourself what those differences are. Now raise both legs toward your chest, and aim both feet at the ceiling, and hold onto the backs of both knees. Once again bob your legs toward your body, very easily, and breathe easily and let your head rest. With your head as it is, turn your eyes to the left and to the right while you're bobbing your legs. Just the eyeballs move. And now roll your head. And rest. Give yourself a minute to experience any differences you feel between now and when we started.

I feel as if I've lost fifty pounds.
I feel sad.
My right leg is about a foot longer than my left.

Turn around now so that your head is toward the center of our circle, and we can put pillows under people's knees. Raise your arms up so that you can look at your hands. Look at the fingers. See what difference there is between one hand and the other. Now look at your partner's hand, next to you. Compare your hand with his or her hand. Are the fingers longer or shorter? Is the color different? The texture of the skin? Turn the hands over—if you've been looking at the backs, look at the palms. First look at your own, then at your partner's. Look at the differences between your own hands and those of your partner. Now clasp your hands together; now put your hands down by your sides; now close your eyes and see what you feel.

What I'd like to do is go into the breathing. If you have anything tight around your waist, loosen it; make yourself as comfortable as you can before we get started. Then I'd like your palms up, if it feels comfortable for you that way.

I'd like you to concentrate on your belly. Just see if you can put your attention on your belly. Let your belly rise as much as it will—don't push it, just let it rise. You might imagine a big balloon 'way down in your belly. As you take in a breath, that balloon blows up in your belly, and as you exhale, the balloon deflates.

Put your right hand down low on your belly, on your lower abdomen, about an inch above your pelvic bone. Let your hand rise and fall as you breathe. Don't *make* it happen, you can always *force* those muscles out. Just see if you can gently coax yourself. Now put your other hand on your chest. I'd like you to make that hand rise and fall as you breathe. Forget about the lower hand, just work on your upper one. See how fully you can breathe into your chest, so it really rises as you breathe. Now breathe into your belly first, and then into your chest, and then exhale. Sigh on the exhalation. Into the belly, up into the chest, and exhale: a-a-a-ah-h-h-h. Repeat this several times. Let your hands fall down to your sides and continue breathing as you're breathing now, while you focus your mind on a triangle. I want the point of the triangle to be up. See if you can see the triangle in your mind's eye. Color it if you wish. Continue to focus on your breathing. I'm going to give you images to look at, but I don't want you to lose this breathing with the belly and chest and exhalation.

What I'd like you to do is to go back to a time when you were fifty years old. You might see who you were with around that time. What people were in your life? If you were working during that time, what kinds of things were you doing in your work? See yourself as clearly as you can: your face, your arms, your legs. See if you can get a clear picture of yourself. I'd like you to see how you feel about that picture. What was it like for you, looking back on it now? What was that time like for you?

Let's move back to age forty. Try to reconstruct what you were doing in your work, who were some of the main characters in your life, the people you lived your life with—who were they? I want you to get a picture of yourself at that age, and then see how you feel about yourself at that age, looking back from now. What was that age like for you? Keep focusing on your breathing. If you lose touch with the pictures in your mind, keep focusing on your breathing. Your breathing is what is going to keep you centered. Full breaths.

Let's go back to age twenty-five. What was your life like at twenty-five? What were your daily activities? Who were some of the main characters in your life? How did you look at that age? How do you feel about yourself at that age from your perspective now? What was life like for you?

I'd like you to go back to your graduation from high school. What was that like? See if you can see any of your classmates in your mind's eye. What was the inside of your school building like? Do you see any teachers? Do you see their faces in your mind? How did you feel about yourself? When you look back from now to high school graduation, what was life like then for you?

I'd like you to change size in your mind. What was the earliest time you can remember? Two? Three? Four? Some time when you were smaller than you are as an adult. See if you can go back to that time. See your parents as they might·have been when you were very young. Maybe brothers and sisters, somebody who was around a lot. And now ask yourself the question, "What did I feel at that age?" What was your life like to you then, looking back from your age now? What was it like to be a really small child?

Breathe into your belly and up into your chest and say a-a-a-a-ah-h-h-h. Again. And a third time. And now begin to stretch out like a cat. Stretch into your feet, and as you come back down to resting, really see what it is to feel, to take all of you in, from the earliest time you can remember all the way up to now. Be with that experience for a few minutes.

APPENDIX B
The SAGE Way

Since 1974, under the auspices of the SAGE Project, groups of older people have been meeting to practice yoga, deep breathing, Tai Chi, biofeedback, autogenics, meditation, touching and massage, guided fantasy, visualization, gestalt exercises, art therapy, and other relaxation, flexibility, and awareness techniques. The results have been revolutionary. In the words of one participant, "Since I've been coming to this group I have made peace with my being old. I see myself as okay for the first time in many years."

SAGE was founded by Gay Gaer Luce, a science writer with a Ph.D. in psychology. Gay has a long-standing interest in sleep and body rhythms, topics she explored in her best-selling books, *Sleep*, *Insomnia*, and *Body Time* (see bibliography).

In 1971, Gay's seventy-year-old mother, Fay Gaer, was having trouble sleeping after a long plane trip. She and Gay experimented with biofeedback and breathing techniques to see if they could bring her relief. She soon learned to relax and fall easily into sleep. Out of this experience, Gay began to speculate about creating an ongoing program designed to counteract the negative effects our cultural concepts have on aging. She discussed the idea with her friend, Eugenia Gerrard, who is a professional marriage and family counselor. Eugenia's interest in working with older people came from seeing her mother suffer from a debilitating illness that put her in nursing homes while she was still in her fifties. Together, the two women decided to launch an exploratory program for people over sixty.

Working with names suggested by their own friends and acquaintances, Gay and Eugenia found a dozen people in their late sixties and early seventies who were willing to commit themselves to the project for six months. These people became SAGE's first "core group."

The core group met in Gay's living room for three hours a week starting in January, 1974. A few months later, Ken Dychtwald, a specialist in self-exploration and development practices with a Ph.D. in psychology, joined the two women as a new co-director of SAGE.

In addition to the group meetings, each member of the group met on a weekly basis with one of the directors to work on exercises and techniques tailored to his or her particular needs. These exercises dealt with matters ranging from arthritis to chronic depression. Core group members also had homework to do: balancing and breathing exercises were stressed, as was "self-expression"—two to four people sharing their intimate experiences of aging with each other; for example, those of being old, of experiencing satisfaction in old age, or of postponing happiness in their lives from youth to middle age to old age.

Guest speakers addressed the group on topics that ranged from ways to improve one's vision to psychic healing and out-of-body experiences; from the relation between mind and body to control of the autonomic nervous system.

Participation in SAGE's core groups was not always a happy or an easy experience. SAGE is a process of self exploration, and often people had to face their deepest fears in order to grow beyond them. Yet, group members found themselves stimulated and challenged. They found that their health improved, that they became more active in their communities, and that they began to discover the depths of their own sensitivity, courage, ability, and personal power in ways they had never imagined before. Rather than disband at the end of the six-month agreement, the members of the group decided to continue their weekly meetings. For two years they met on a weekly basis; then, in April, 1976—with Gay, Eugenia, and Ken coping with the increasing demands of a growing organization—Core Group I moved out on its own, and later began to meet once a week with Core Group II as The SAGE Community.

Presently there are eight core groups, consisting of people who are financially self-sufficient. Most members are white and middle-class, and though some of them feel a money pinch, none is dependent on other people for day-to-day support. Early in its work with the core groups, the SAGE staff became confident that the program worked in this relatively independent environment. Older people living in institutions present a different kind of challenge.

During its first year, SAGE received a grant from the Oakland (California) Public Library's Project Outreach, which allowed it to move into several senior residences and convalescent hospitals. The people in these institutions were relatively deprived. Many were confined to wheelchairs, many were severely depressed, and many had long ceased trying to communicate with anyone about anything.

Response to the SAGE program in these institutions was neither as spectacular nor as immediate as it had been with the core groups. But at the end of an initial ten-week trial period, institution residents had begun to show a marked interest in the program, as well as a renewed interest in their own lives, and the SAGE institutional program began to attract attention and support from senior residences, institutions, and hospitals throughout the country. Funded by various grants, SAGE has continued its institutional work.

Although SAGE rarely sought publicity, and never recruited new members except by word of mouth, newspapers and national magazines—including the *New York Times, Human Behavior,* the *New Age Journal, Modern Maturity,* and *California Living*—began to seek out SAGE. As more and more people heard about SAGE and its alternative approaches to dealing with the problems of aging, the project's directors were inundated with requests for interviews and lecture appearances. Videotapes recording the SAGE experience and specific SAGE techniques circulated widely among professionals and other people interested in the field of aging.

Meanwhile, SAGE began a series of workshops to share its methods with other interested groups. Ken travelled throughout the country conducting these workshops and giving lectures. Training became almost as important an activity within SAGE as leading the groups or working in institutions.

The SAGE program is characterized by a holistic approach to health. A person's problems are not divided into arbitrary categories such as "mental" or "physical." SAGE's focus is on the complexity of the human individual and his or her well-being. SAGE makes no assumption that anyone is "sick" or "needs help" or has "a problem." SAGE emphasizes "wellness," the well-being and harmony of the whole person: body, mind, emotions, and spirit. SAGE sees each man and each woman as a work of highest creation, and not simply a collection of disparate parts thrown together into a body-machine.

As the holistic approach constitutes one of SAGE's major premises, so does personal responsibility, which entails the idea that each of us creates his or her own health and illness. This notion of responsibility does not suggest that illness is imaginary, but rather that it is a message from the body that something in a person's life is out of balance and ought to be examined.

SAGE also stresses attention to the individual here and now: the program does not proceed through a rigid schedule of exercises at a forced pace, but works on an individual basis, accepting a person's beliefs and feelings and progressing from that point. It is an approach that encourages people to try new ideas without pressure. SAGE emphasizes experience, not technique. For example, the point is not whether a Tai Chi exercise is executed with classical precision, but how it feels to the individual doing it.

Nothing in yoga, autogenics, gestalt, or any of the other SAGE techniques is inherently alien to the aged. The techniques are simply tools that can be used flexibly to enhance a person's well-being at any age. One has only to watch a group of elderly Chinese practicing Tai Chi in a park in the cold morning light, or see films of Fritz Perls conducting an encounter session, to recognize that, while aging is a reality, its effects need not fit our limited and limiting cultural stereotypes.

For the majority of older Americans, the practical and psychological barriers to active participation in the kinds of activities SAGE utilizes are prohibitive. Most groups that practice these techniques meet on schedules or at locations that make it physically difficult for older people to have access to them. More importantly, older people often express their reluctance to "intrude" on the activities of younger people. And many younger people, in their turn, shy away from the aged with a kind of blind fear—perhaps of their own futures.

In part, it is SAGE's purpose to break through the artificial barriers that isolate people and prevent them from being vibrantly alive in old age. Participants in SAGE have witnessed remarkable changes in their lives. Perhaps the most important of these is that they feel more satisfied and fulfilled. They are more accepting of themselves as they are. They have grown to like themselves more than they used to, and to find new dimensions of themselves to enjoy. For themselves, and for the rest of us as well, they have become sages indeed.

Anyone who is interested in further particulars about SAGE should contact the organization directly:

> SAGE
> Claremont Office Park
> 41 Tunnel Road
> Berkeley, CA 94705
> (415) 841-9858

In addition, Ken Dychtwald has formed the National Association for Humanistic Gerontology (NAHG). NAHG operates as a nation-wide organization to share resources, and to support and stimulate a humanistic approach to gerontology. It also is preparing a list of other groups around the United States that are working with older people in a manner similar to the SAGE way. Anyone interested in learning what SAGE-oriented organizations exist in his or her own community should contact Ken at NAHG, whose address is the same as SAGE's, above.

BIOGRAPHIES

Gay Gaer Luce is a psychologist and former science writer whose investigations into the psychology of insomnia led her to disturbing conclusions about drug-based therapies. As a result, she studied techniques for relaxation such as meditation, hypnosis, and biofeedback. She continued to move away from scholarly research and began to work directly with people as a co-director of SAGE. She is presently writing a history of SAGE which will include how-to-do-it exercises for older people.

Eugenia Gerrard grew up in a small Texas town, and was trained in dance. She was a dance therapist before doing graduate work in psychology. She is a licensed marriage and family counselor. After four years as a co-director of SAGE, she looks forward to "retiring" herself, and plans to direct her energies inward, as a wife and mother of three children, aged 19, 17, and 14.

Paul Preuss

Ken Dychtwald is a humanistic psychologist who has been a student and teacher of yoga for nine years. He is a former Esalen Institute seminar leader. In addition to his current work as a co-director of SAGE, he is Founding President of the National Association for Humanistic Gerontology, and serves as a consultant and adjunct instructor at numerous colleges and universities.

Karen Preuss holds a B.A. from the University of Chicago, and an M.A. in anthropology from the University of Washington. She spent a year with an anthropological team in the highlands of New Guinea before taking up photography on Kodiak Island, Alaska. As a freelance photographer her work has appeared in *Human Behavior, New West, Horizon,* and many other publications. She was one of twelve photographers chosen by the State of California for the *California Workers* project in 1975. She regards her training in anthropology as excellent preparation for her work in documentary photography, which she sees primarily as a means of communication among and about people.

BIBLIOGRAPHY

Articles about SAGE

Ansley, Helen G., "A New Life at 76," *Modern Maturity* (October/November, 1976).

Beyers, Charlotte K., "The Holistic Medicine Show," *San Francisco Magazine* (July, 1976).

Dychtwald, Ken, "SAGE and NAHG: Creating a New Image of Aging," *Yoga Journal* (January, 1976).

———— "The SAGE Project: A New Image of Aging," *Journal of Humanistic Psychology* (April, 1978).

Ellie & Margaret & Mac & Alice & a Few Others, "Talking about SAGE," *Noetic News* (Spring, 1976).

Elwell, C. C. II, "The SAGE Spirit," *Human Behavior* (March, 1976).

Fields, Suzanne, "The Greening of Old Age: SAGE Can Be a Spice of Life," *Innovations* (Spring, 1977).

Houston, Jean, "The Elderly Are Not Obsolete," *New York Times Special Features* (May 25, 1975).

Kendall, Adelaide, "SAGE," in The Berkeley Holistic Health Center, *The Holistic Health Handbook*. Berkeley: And/Or, 1978.

Laughingbird, "SAGE," *New Age Journal* (January, 1975).

———— "The SAGE Project: New Life in Old Age," *Berkeley Monthly* (December 2, 1976).

McDonald, Worden, "An Old Guy Who Feels Good," *California Living* (November 28, 1976).

Prosser, Adelaide, in "And Some Voices from Out Here," *Human Behavior* (July, 1977).

Books by SAGE People

Dychtwald, Ken, *Bodymind*. New York: Pantheon, 1977.

Luce, Gay Gaer, *Body Time*. New York: Pantheon, 1971.

Luce, Gay Gaer, and Segal, Julius, *Insomnia: the Guide for the Troubled Sleeper*. New York: Doubleday, 1969.

———— *Sleep*. New York: Coward, McCann & Geoghegan, 1966.

McDonald, Worden, *An Old Guy Who Feels Good*. Berkeley: Thorpe Springs, 1978.

Books Recommended by SAGE Directors

Arguelles, J., and Arguelles, M., *Mandala*. Berkeley: Shambhala, 1972.

Assagioli, R., *Psychosynthesis*. New York: Viking, 1971.

Baker, E., *Man in the Trap*. New York: Avon, 1967.

Bonny, H., and Savary, L., *Music and Your Mind*. New York: Harper & Row, 1973.

Brooks, C., *Sensory Awareness*. New York: Viking, 1974.

Brown, B., *New Mind, New Body*. New York: Harper & Row, 1974.

Bucke, R. M., *Cosmic Consciousness*. New York: Dutton, 1969.

Campbell, J., *Myths to Live By*. New York: Bantam, 1973.

Casteneda, C., *The Teachings of Don Juan*. New York: Ballantine, 1968.

———— *A Separate Reality*. New York: Simon & Schuster, 1971.

———— *Journey to Ixtlan*. New York: Simon & Schuster, 1972.

———— *Tales of Power*. New York: Simon & Schuster, 1974.

Curtin, S., *Nobody Ever Died of Old Age*. Boston: The Atlantic Monthly Press.

DeBeauvoir, S., *The Coming of Age*. New York: Putnam, 1972.

De Ropp, R. S., *The Master Game*. New York: Putnam, 1972.

De Vries, H. A., *Vigor Regained*. Englewood Cliffs, New Jersey: Prentice-Hall, 1974.

Downing, G., *Massage*. New York: Bookworks/Random House, 1974.

Faraday, A., *The Dream Game*. New York: Harper and Row, 1974.

Feldenkrais, M., *Awareness Through Movement*. New York: Harper & Row, 1972.

Geba, B., *Breathe Away Your Tension*. New York: Bookworks/Random House, 1973.

———— *Vitality Training for Older Adults*. New York: Bookworks/Random House, 1972.

Govinda, Lama, A., *The Way of the White Clouds*. Berkeley: Shambhala, 1966.

Gunther, B., *Sense Relaxation: Below Your Mind.* New York: Collier, 1968.

Jung, C. G., *Memories, Dreams, Reflections.* New York: Vintage/Knopf/Random House, 1961.

Keleman, S., *Your Body Speaks Its Mind.* New York: Simon & Schuster, 1975.

——— *Living Your Dying.* New York: Bookworks/Random House, 1974.

Kubler-Ross, E., *On Death and Dying.* New York: Macmillan, 1969.

LeShan, L., *How to Meditate.* New York: Bantam, 1975.

Maslow, A., *Toward a Psychology of Being.* New York: Van Nostrand Reinhold, 1968.

Mishlove, J., *The Roots of Consciousness.* New York: Bookworks/Random House, 1975.

Monroe, R., *Journeys Out of the Body.* New York: Doubleday, 1972.

Ornstein, R. F. *The Psychology of Consciousness.* San Francisco: Freeman, 1972.

Oyle, I., *The Healing Mind.* Millbrae: Celestial Arts, 1974.

Pearce, J. C., *The Crack in the Cosmic Egg.* New York: Julian, 1971.

Roberts, J., *The Nature of Personal Reality.* Englewood Cliffs, New Jersey: Prentice-Hall, 1974.

Samuels, M., and Nancy, S., *Seeing with the Mind's Eye.* New York: Bookworks/Random House, 1975.

Samuels, M., and Bennett, H., *The Well Body Book.* New York: Bookworks/Random House, 1973.

Satchidananda, S., *Integral Yoga Hatha.* New York: Holt, Rinehart and Winston, 1970.

Schutz, W., *Joy.* New York: Grove Press, 1967.

Selye, H., *Stress Without Distress.* Philadelphia: Lippincott, 1976.

Suzuki, S., *Zen Mind, Beginner's Mind.* New York: Weatherhill, 1970.

Trungpa, C., *Meditation in Action.* Berkeley: Shambhala, 1970.

Tarthang, T., *Gesture of Balance.* Berkeley: Dharma, 1977.

——— *Space, Time, and Knowledge.* Berkeley: Dharma, 1978.

Ulene, A., *Feeling Fine.* Los Angeles: J. P. Tarcher, 1977.

Vishnudevenanda, S., *The Complete Illustrated Book of Yoga.* New York: Julian, 1960.

Watts, A., *Psychotherapy East and West.* New York: Mentor, 1963.

——— *The Spirit of Zen.* New York: Grove Press, 1958.

Typesetting: Chapman's Phototypesetting
Copy editing and proofreading: Mark Malkas
Camera work: Art Graphics, Berkeley
Printing: Joel Shefflin at Peter G. Levison Associates,
    San Francisco/Fremont Litho
Type: 11/14 Aster with Italic
Paper: 80 lb. Shasta Suede
Halftones: 1 color (black), 150-220 duoline screen